Sandpaper

Sandpaper

a collection of poetry by Ravenn L. Moore

**PAPERTHICK
PUBLISHING**™

Sandpaper © 2017 by Ravenn L. Moore

All rights reserved. No part of this book may be reproduced or transmitted in any form or by any means, whatsoever, without prior written permission of the publisher. Requests for permission should be directed to Paperthick Publishing LLC.

ISBN (hardcover): 978-0-9992467-0-2

ISBN (paperback): 978-0-9992467-1-9

ISBN (e-book): 978-0-9992467-2-6

Library of Congress Control Number: 2017918836

Published by:
Paperthick Publishing LLC
Detroit, MI
www.paperthickpublishing.com
www.facebook.com/PaperthickPublishing

Copy Editor: Valerie A. Congdon
Book cover and design: Rose Lowry, Beechleaf Design

First edition, 2017

Words will never suffice
Words will never conjure the call
Words will never justify the sacrifice
Words will never describe how you love me, as best you can
Thank you, Mommy and Daddy

PARTICLES

Prologue xvi
Epigraph: Coffee Shop xix

Part I: EXTRA COARSE GRIT
    Ode to coiffures........................2
    Desperate..............................4
    Boredom stole..........................5
    U-turn.................................6
    Out of spaces..........................7
    Running................................8
    Boxed in...............................9
    Path of no return 10
    Push 11
    My cool............................... 12
    Almost over 13
    Resistance 14
    Heaviness 16
    Scream 17
    Rainbow............................... 18
    Inside 19
    My strong............................. 20
    Live 21
    Take charge 22
    Bending knee 23
    Waiting............................... 24
    Wunderstand 25
    Church 26
    Stigma 28

Part II: COARSE GRIT

Torture 32
Subsequently 33
Last time 34
Stripped 35
Settling.................................... 36
Ready 37
Agility...................................... 38
Cumbersome............................ 39
Unconscious 41
My heart aches 42
Residue 43
What am I to do? 44
I'm not ready for you to leave.......... 46
Still 47
Abandoned 48
Funny thing is... 50
Give me another chance 51
Invisible.................................. 52
Heartbreaker............................ 53
How did I get here? 54
How do I survive unrequited love?..... 56
I need you 57
I should be over you................. 58
Idea of love 60
Introduction 61
Leave....................................... 62
Leftover 64
A 66
Stay... 67
It_hurts@forward..................... 68
I'm not 69

No commitment 70
Train wreck 72
Flower brigade 74
Traffic light 75
Let me go! 76

Part III: MEDIUM GRIT

Henceforth. 80
In due time 81
Inward 84
Love again 85
I thought it was me 86
Not #1. 87
Expectations 88
Unfaithful 89
When you gone. 90
What do you want from me? 91
Analogy 92
Love you in wonderment 93
55 days in. 95
Dreams birthed. 97
Don't forget love 98

Part IV: FINE GRIT

Sit-in 102
Onward. 103
Clutter. 104
Grandeur 105
Giving. 106
Significance. 110
Moving on 111

Believe in me.................... 112
I am single..................... 113
Chill........................... 114
Conscious....................... 115
You get to there................. 116
Figure it out.................... 118
Love circle 119
Peace........................... 121

Part V: EXTRA FINE GRIT

New............................ 124
What is this love?............... 125
Scars........................... 127
Freestyle....................... 128
Reach!.......................... 129
At the heart of it 130
Dream cloud 131
Fellowship 132
Saturday........................ 133
I've got to get to You, God 134
Growth 135
Wonder......................... 136
The words 137
I look for You.................... 138

Epilogue: May 141
Inspiration for book title 143
Dedication 145
About the author.................... 147
Acknowledgments 148

PROLOGUE

Why *Sandpaper?* Because of its parallels to life. Take, for example, sandpaper has a rough surface and is rubbed against something to remove surface material to make the surface either smoother or rougher. The rough surface or abrasive material in sandpaper has a particle size which is referred to as grit size. Grit sizes go from higher-grade grit (extra coarse to coarse) to lower-grade grit (medium to extra fine). In the process of sanding an object you start with a higher-grade grit (extra coarse) for the toughest surfaces and end the process with a lower-grade grit (extra fine) for final polishing. This is a lot like life to me. The use of sandpaper on an object to make its' surface smoother or rougher is like building resiliency as you journey through the tests of life.

The different grades of grit embedded in the sandpaper are analogous to the different tests of life. The surface material removed during sanding can be a myriad of things from heartache and loss to old beliefs and habits that both test and teach us about life and the human condition, and illuminate more of who we are at the core. That which is removed is marked by growth; how you've grown, what you have learned and endured from the tests of life. What remains after the sanding is resilience, revelatory depth, levels of emotion, and understanding; each circuitously develops character.

The actual rubbing or sanding is the Creator's design for our lives, what we need to learn to get to the next level, or to get to the next grit. As the tests of life rub, the dead parts fall like dust or ashes and we shine brighter, more beautifully. Therefore, each poem in *Sandpaper* is categorized by grits; indicating the level of sanding that took place to unveil the depth and level of emotion experienced in each poem.

The poems in *Sandpaper* enlist a level of complexity and levels of emotion but don't necessarily reflect one situation, circumstance or person. The poems are not personal accounts per se, rather, a collection of processed thoughts and ideas compiling sensory experiences downloaded into poetry form. I want to tap into your emotional circuitry so you feel emotions you may not have felt before reading *Sandpaper*. Likewise, every time I read *Sandpaper*, I experience a different emotion too.

Through reading *Sandpaper*, I hope you explore and discover a depth and level of emotion that is new or symbiotic. We are all connected in some way. This collection of poetry is truly a reflection of the human condition by which we feel, touch, hear, smell and see life in many layers and manners and states. If you feel emotions – new or resonant – reading each poem, we've connected on an inexplicable level. With that said, I am excited to share with you, *Sandpaper!*

EPIGRAPH

Coffee shop

I kept looking up from my book because it felt like someone was looking at me but I didn't fix my gaze on any particular passenger on the train. It was a full cart this morning. As I was getting off the train, I felt a strong gaze on my neck and subtly turned around to a gushing smile of sorts. "Wow! You are glowing," he said. "Thank you," I intoned. Much to my consternation, imbued by the agency of my already suspicious nature, he continued as if we were familiar acquaintances. "What do you eat? What do you use?" Before responding, I thought to myself what kind of questions are these to ask a stranger? I must have paused for more seconds than I counted because he continued without my answers to his questions. "It's just that I've noticed your transformation over the past few months and I had to say something," he said. I gave a wry smile with slight intrigue and still considerable suspicion. He and I took the same route to work for a year or so, I had noticed him occasionally but we never exchanged subtleties or even small talk until today.

I thought the conversation had trailed off but he seemed to be walking in the same direction as me, toward the coffee shop up the street. He ensued, "If you tell me your skin regimen, your coffee is on me." "Free coffee," I retorted as I glanced over him for the first time really. I obliged. He was cute! There was no band on his ring finger either.

Once we got to the coffee shop, I spotted a table near the window and offered to hold seats for us while he went to place our order. "I'll have a small coconut milk latte please," I said. And in the same breath I reminded him, "I'm not sure of this transformation you're referring to but I can share with you what I eat and what I use on my skin." He said, "I am really interested. You look amazing." We exchanged chuckles. As he walked away, I could tell that he took great care of himself. He was very fit, smelled of lavender, manicured nails – just a polished guy from head to toe so I was even more bewildered by his inclination for *my* skin regimen. I muddled over what I had done in the past few months, to my recollection nothing had changed. Then I thought, 'Aha!'

When he returned with our coffees, he was surprised to see a book on the table. "What's that?" he said. "This is my skin regimen," I said. "Huh? You're really going to have to explain this to me," he said. I smiled coyly and said: "When the going gets tough, the tough get going. This I have found to be true. When you've crowded your life with ashes or deadweight there is no room for you; there is no room for beauty, no room for joy, no room for praise. When there is no room left for you in your life, at that moment, the tough stuff truly gets going. Now I am making room for me again." He still looked perplexed.

I thought to myself how in the past few months I ended the notion that life as of now could have been any different. Before I thought maybe if I was better, maybe if I tried harder, maybe if I was someone else, maybe if I didn't get depressed, and just maybe if I had been stronger, life wouldn't have gotten the best of me. Up until now I thought I had done something wrong to end up *here*.

As I was going through the tests of life, I didn't know how to deal with the emotions of life, for I had not developed coping skills. Life was happening to me, not for me. The disappointments of life, and what I thought was failure at the time, was in fact a necessary part of my journey. When I gathered my writings, some on old crumpled store receipts, some on balled up pieces of paper, or tucked away in notebooks, journals and old emails, I saw something different.

I thought I only saw loss or failure or rejection. But what was most apparent were my emotions written out on paper, the rawness and vulnerability that I fought tooth and nail to suppress because they were uncomfortable, unfamiliar. Once written down on paper I could see my emotions for the first time, not the specific situation or specific circumstance, and it was a beautiful sight to behold. Simply put, life is meant to be felt and experienced, and emotions are the conduits to feel life, all of it.

The Creator's design for my life sanded away the deadweight so that I could see the emotions instead. The dust that overlay my emotions, once I was no longer suppressing, avoiding or uncomfortable, I was able to blow off the dust and what was left when the dust settled, was beauty. The words read like oil and clothed the paper with a sense of honor, a license for living that only age, time, experience, understanding and wisdom can certificate.

"I've found my way back," I said juxtaposed with our conversation and my self-talk. I simply told him, "God gave me beauty for my ashes, here is the account." He gave me a puzzled look and before he could speak, I said, "Here is your own copy of *Sandpaper*. Enjoy!"

Part I: EXTRA COARSE GRIT

Sandpaper with Extra Coarse Grit is used for sanding and stripping the toughest surfaces.

Ode to coiffures

Freedom rings, as I call them because I can do the dandiest things; like swim or play or workout or vacation, however or whenever I want. That's also why I call them coils more often than freedom rings or my freedom ringlets.

My coils, hidden beneath it all have a sense of resiliency about them: the spoils of time past, the hatred, the anger, the shame, so much to discover within each springing bounce, being pushed down but rising again with even more fervor and flare. Some call it a hiding spot for watermelon seed or even okra and bobby pens or writing pens.

Nonetheless my coils have been suppressed, then unearthed and sometimes even undone. Why you ask? Well, you see, because it reminds too many of too much and not enough of beauty in the winding of the thing. There is that coil. Ooh, chile let me find some steam, some heat or something so it doesn't frame me raggedly.

Aah, my coil is gone for now but it'll be back, no matter what I do, in a few weeks, a month or two. Then I looked again, I must've missed one, where did it go—well, well I don't know why it reminds too many of too much and not enough of beauty in the winding of the thing—there is that coil.

This coil is so soft and unique, can't buy these coils, my coil is home grown, and it grows with its own agenda, and no two are alike. As much as I try, I can't control the thing, there is that coil, how does it do such things? It bounces, has a life and a mind of its own—now isn't that what beauty is to begin with—unharnessed, yet ripe, self-efficacy…withstanding torment, torture, heat, burn, blood, pain, blows, tugs, tight pulls, grabbing, hatred spewed from the eye of the beholder, even the eye in the mirror and they say my coil ain't beautiful.

I just don't understand why it reminds too many of too much and not enough of beauty in the winding of the thing. Come to think of it, the only thing not beautiful is my questioning God—crying, disgusted, pleading, begging for something different while changing it, hiding it, ignoring it and with lack of air, suffocating my coils—asking God, why did you give me this hair? And God responds to my heart, because your coils are like *My* coils and what if I gave you that part of *Me*?

I smile and quickly make peace with 'why it reminds too many of too much and not enough of beauty in the winding of the thing.' Look at my coils.

Desperate

How pathetic
I still chase the idea of you
At this threshold of desperation
And regret
Your shadow will do
So where am I now?
Outside my purpose
I can't quiet it in my head
And no remedy or resolution is in sight
Bills, worldly responsibilities tantamount
And I'm stuck
All behaviors, bad behaviors with consequences
Louder than the disdain
Creating new focal points
New worries
New distractions
Health risks, overweight, underweight, self-loathing
Pale in comparison to living a life outside my purpose
If not truth, then what have you?
If not water, then what sustains you?
Without love, then what are you?
Without peace, then what keeps you?
Without purpose, then what fate may become of you?
The disdain is so loud it hurts
Tears watering an empty pot with no dream to sprout
A flood rising on the inside
No roots to nourish

Boredom stole

Isn't it kinda mean how boredom can steal a dream

Turn a nice day into waste

Wouldn't it be liberating if I could determine the productivity I needed

To take advantage of a day with so many possibilities

Instead I've gotta work a no-end job and it hurts

My creativity lurks to no avail again

So I'm twiddling my thumbs trying to daydream away the dumb

Still trying to conceal the frustration

So my heart turns numb

Because I know somebody is discovering and inventing and creating this afternoon

But I'll be patient because after this boredom subsides

I'll be doing something worthwhile too

U-turn

Every road I've taken
I've had to turn around
Take the best route
Without mistake
And pretend to be all right
But any road I take is the way to go
For no man really knows
Until you've gone where no one has gone
Until you push yourself so far along
There is no turning back

Out of spaces

I'm running out of spaces to run
Every second lived untrue
Is making me come undone
I'm unraveling at the seams
Trying to run through the open spaces
So I can scream
My dreams aren't good enough
Romantic love can't meet the touch
I've even run out of vices
I don't have a crutch
I'm running out of spaces to run
Every second lived untrue
Is making me come undone
I want to dance away the worry
I want to breathe away the wrong turns
I want to push through the challenges
I want to live
And live truthfully
I want to give my all
Even when it hurts
I'm running out of spaces to run…

Running

I'm running
From something real fast

Maybe it's that look in your eyes
Or your words that make me cry
Or the feeling you give me
That reminds me of every insecurity
And the stereotypes that cage me
The fears inside
I can't deny

I'm running
From something real fast

Boxed in

I want to run where
No one can catch me
I want to dance to an inner beat
No one else can hear
I want to experience the sun
Until I can't be seen
I want to get so close to the edge
That my destiny is brimming
Push away the draining things
Kick off life's boundaries
Shove away life's boundaries
Shove away hate, self-pity and envy
Hold on to love and humility
Then run to the open spaces
Where your head is clear
Running fast
Just to be free in the open spaces
Where you can breathe, just be!

Path of no return

It's the path of no return
My ambition has carried me thus far
I've grown so much
Now I look back and the gap is vast
Between those I once knew, before
Those I love
And those that love me, still
And the knowledge gap is so wide
I can't go back
I don't even know how to go back
I feel stuck and uneven and sad
It's the path of no return
I don't know how to love across the gap
I can't reach that far back
That means love is in the past
And there is no present love
Is knowledge that powerful?
Should I have opted only for understanding?
Is knowledge the path of no return?
But I don't believe in regrets…
Hello acceptance.

Push

It's an invisible cage

With a force stronger than gravity

It's painful to say the least

The vision you're striving for is clear as day

In that place just beyond your grasp, your reach

For some reason each reach is more tiring

As if the vision embodies inertia

That the reach, and each subsequent is from an exhausted place

Wheels spinning

Wondering when that moment,

When that moment of energy will propel me toward the vision

Birthed in my mind

My cool

My body is singing the blues
No one is playing by the rules
I ain't got the ordinary tools
I've been blinded searching for cues
My experiences paid my dues
I am a smart fool
This oxymoron disrupts my mood
I'm looking for my cool
Clouded by my thoughts
Jaded by my views

Almost over

This

Conjures up emotions these days,

More good than bad...

And I smile, accepting what is...

I share because I own this truth

Acknowledge receipt

At least acknowledge

Even acknowledge you reject it

Just acknowledge

There's no judgment on my end

I need to know you heard me

Resistance

I've resisted everything often

Pushed against the forces of circumstance

Forces of fate

Forces of what is

Forces of now

Forces of ...

I've often resisted love at its ripest moments

I still think of you

I think of you too

Both of you

I resisted that; I can't make the same mistake twice, *twice*

They are not coming back now

So what does the future hold?

I've resisted freedom; insanity

I reach for it; yearn for it with both arms as both feet go in another direction

I even resist that notion

I resist that I can't change it;

Change the hurt to love

Change the disappointment to hope

But I can't, I resist that

I resisted the choices I've made but accept the development that has occurred

I resist my emotions but accept my reaction

Then I resist my reaction but accept the response

I get it

I do

But I resist that notion too

It was good, really, but I resist that too

It's over

I resisted that

You don't get that time back

You don't…

OK I'm sadder now

I'm powerful, limitless, infinite existence; true

But without knowing that I resisted

I hope for better, desire best and pray for excellence

A second chance even

I believe it gets better

Grow, know, learn, and be in the now

Heaviness

I felt the pressure
It hurts
As invisible as it is
The hurt is alive, tangible
Selfishly limiting my breath
Taking space within
An uninvited guest
So I couldn't see it coming
Once it settled
It was too heavy to push away

Scream

Full of steam

Ooh I'm mad

And all I want to do is scream

Yell and holler

I need something to grab

To pull and to tug

I'm madder than a mug

I need to scream

I need to shout

I need to yell about it

I'm angry

So angry

Red angry

Scream!

Shout!

I gotta get it out

Cause I'm angry!

Rainbow

Rainbows, have you?

Yeah what about the languid blue and gray hues?

Do you even have time for me to explain?

Time for me to say more about my pot o' gold and what happened to my reds, purples, yellows, oranges

Because only rain I see, and the sky

But you think I should be happy for my blue and gray hues?

Well, what rainbows have you?

Ooh, me too; blue, dark blue, miniature blue, gigantic blue, oh, and don't forget grey, gray and any other way they spell gray

And we can't leave out heather's gray either

So I have all the blues, greys and sometimes clear

Clear is when the flood or shall I say water covers me up, which by the way,

That's what I thought the rainbow was for – a reminder that there won't be another earth flood

But you know what, I'm missing a few colors anyway

Remember I'm missing yellows, oranges, reds, purples; all of the colors except blues and gray, grey, heather's gray and any other way they spell gray, and clear from the flood rains

There ain't no promise

And there MUST be holes in my rainbow...

Inside

You stop trying

You give up

But there is something inside

That tells you something great is within

So you kick and scream and question the greatness

The magnitude of the greatness scares you

...and scares you

A truth you try to suffocate with vices

But I trust the same Guide that lets me know something great is within

Is the same Guide that lets me overcome the fear and

Drowns my soul with determination to reach for

To strive for

To live in the greatness

My strong

I want to give up
I want to walk away from it all
My dreams are fading away
Defeat trumps
Where'd I go wrong?
What'd I do wrong?
Why am I not strong?
Where is my strong?
I gotta get it together
I gotta pull myself together
Press toward
Press forward
To the next level
To the next revel
Can't stop though that seems the easy route
It'll be hell if I stay here

Live

All of this nonsense

Confusion

By the time I get to being

Being free

Living

Living honestly

Confusion is going to have me tired

So tired

I want to kick something

I want to hit something

Because I want to be something

I want to do something

And I'm tired

But I keep vying

Dying for a time

A moment to live!

Take charge

Take charge they say
You've gotta do something with your life
They don't even know I pray
I want to get it right
But when I try there is a stronghold
I'm choking and dying inside
But I refuse to let go
Be all you can be is a slogan
There's much more to it than that and no one told me
God, I'm longing for your Presence
Some nights I cry to a dry heave
Some nights I pray so long it hurts my knees
Because in this season
I'm learning patience
I still don't know the reason

Bending knee

Stifled by the snares

Confused by the musical chairs

Amused by the gray hairs

Bombarded by the cares

Sensitive because of the tears

Tolerant because of the wear

Hopeful for the repairs

Delighted because I'm rare

Exhausted all swears

No more 'I don't give a damns!'

This load I can't bear

My being cannot be contained like air

Not looking for guidance from a soothsayer or just anywhere

Now I'm on my knees in prayer

Waiting

Prolific

Gifted

Struggling with forgiveness

God fearing

Honest spirited

Scared of parable of the talents

Useful vessel

Loaned wisdom

Sinful, not taking advantage of it

Waitlisted

Hidden

Upset

But God loves me

Yoke broken

Anointing descended

But am I ready to do?

Purging and goading

Beforehand

God will make sure

I'm ready to be fruitful

Wunderstand

I don't understand
I don't wunderstand
Let it go
You don't wanna hear my flow
Does it matter?
Should I care?

Church

I'm in this church
The eulogy, the prayer
And it still hurts
I want them back
Bring them back
The gut wrenching feeling
God, if I make it through this
I need to touch You to get some healing
I want them back
Bring them back
Gone too soon
He was like a big brother
And he was like a little brother
Now they're in the tomb
I want them back
Bring them back
Our neighborhood never had this type of loss
We're all in disbelief
Every hand, holding every face
This can't happen again
I won't let it happen again
Fighting so it won't happen again no matter the cost
We've heard the news before
We watched in horror as it happened to others
200 girls missing from their village

Trayvon Martin

Newtown children

Emilio Hoffman

Listen, we're all connected

We feel the loss and we're all affected

In him I see me

In her I find me

I want them back

Bring them back!

How long will this go on?

We've gotta pull together

There is strength in numbers

Let it guide you, let it help you, let it reveal you, let it rebuild you, let it shield you, let it heal you

Don't let it take you, don't let it change you, don't let it break you

We can handle it

We gotta manage it

Don't carry the heaviness by yourself

Be strong in this;

We all gotta live with the fact

They are not coming back

Stigma

What's your name?
Is that your real name?
"Yes.
Well, I changed it after I checked in
I don't want those closest to me to know I'm in here
They will judge me
And I don't want them to talk about me
Or tell people where I am
No one will care to investigate"
Why not?
"I don't know and that hurts too"
What hurts?
"It hurts too that no one cares…"
How did you get here?
"I checked myself in"
Why?
"I've been hurt a lot"
Physically?
"No"
Verbally?
"A little…"
Why'd you say you've been hurt a lot then?
"Emotionally…a lot"
Do you want to talk about it?
"With you, yes"

Was it a romantic relationship, family or friend that hurt you emotionally?

"All three, and societal"

What's on your mind now?

Anything happen recently?

"There's a lot"

Well let's start from the beginning...

Okay?

"OK"

Part II: COARSE GRIT

Sandpaper with Coarse Grit is used for heavy sanding and stripping, or roughing a surface.

Torture

Whether with you or apart
It feels like torture
Legally bound
Sweet painful
Your love is out of control
When it leaves you
It runs rampant
My heart must've been a bullseye
Because your love tortures me
Day and night
It's so sporadic
Many highs
But too low, lows
It's just like torture
It hurts until I've had enough
And when I come up for air
Even for a moment
I suffocate again from your love
Electric shocks through my body
Pain of your love has my heart captive
But without it
I have no pulse
You're a love line and a hearse
How can loving you bring me to life and bury me alive?

Subsequently

I needed you for a time, for this moment
My grasp was unreal, firm and eternal
I was afraid to let go
A part of you kept me from falling apart, again
The agony of wonderment in the spaces of time
When I didn't know where you were
Where you stood
What you wanted
Deep down I knew it was temporal
But if I ever challenged myself to be in the moment
It was with you
How painful and humanly illuminating
The oxymoron of wanting forever for a short while
I felt your purpose in my life fleeting
I entered into this like raging waters into an abyss
Saddened, yet alive for the moment
The feeling like no other
No tourniquet to isolate or stop the drain
The love cells unrequited, sending life to the pain
Because in the moment, though you were leaving from the time you came
I was alive

Last time

"This isn't good for us, but I can't say no"
And I can't let go
Why did you even pick up?
"I don't know"
Tell me no
"It's just not a good idea"
You still live there?
"Hurry up"
Don't rush me
"This is the last time"
I know,
I know.

Stripped

You're leaving me and there's nothing I can do
The way we made love
Afterward
The way you sat up
The look in your eyes
...I knew
This was the last time
I'd be in your arms
It's complicated
Neither of us done wrong
But my senses are alert
My heart is on alarm
You're leaving me and there's nothing I can do
I'm not sure how we got here
I was silent when I should've said words
You did things that lifted my guard
Love was here
Rare love
Real love
For some strange reason, that's not enough
You're leaving me and there's nothing I can do
If I ever heal from this
If I ever learn to deal with it
Love will exist again
Even if it is without us two
You're leaving me and there's nothing I can do
Oh, heart
I didn't guard you
And there's nothing I can do

Settling

I don't even have all of you
The piece of you that I have
Funny thing is
It fills something I'm missing
I'm settling
Emotionally I'm still empty
Addicted to suffering
Because love as I know it
Always hurt
I can't walk away
Not right now
I like the suffering
It's still one less empty tank of mine
And that's enough, for now

Ready

"I am ready for love

Why are you hiding from me?" India Arie.

That's what my mouth says

But my actions tell something different

Been alone for so long

I forgot the ins and outs of love

My subtle attempt to flirt

Is thwarted by a memory of the hurt

The rejection palpable

But the longing for love is overwhelming

So what am I to do?

I'm ready for love

But my actions tell another

The crushing feeling when an open heart

Is closed by a no or rejection or fear of falling a part

Agility

You left me to deal
With the introduction of a new emotion to my system
Lost.
I don't know where to go from here
I've been lost ever since you let me go
Forever.
This emotion will always be here, it seems
I'd never felt this emotion before you
Who?
You gotta know who you are
And what you did to my heart
I'll never be the same
You...

Cumbersome

Love doesn't tell time
Many years later, still
There are only two I ever wanted to marry
They didn't choose me
Well, he forgot how we once loved
He forgot how much he could be himself around me
Often I would remind him
I would say, "Hey! It's me"
Moments later the conversation would change
And he wouldn't keep me at the distance
He kept me when we started the conversation
We've talked about this before
But in the past...
The other one
Well, I supposedly got closure years ago
This is why I'm not really "still there"
No one has compared
He told me I was lazy
He wanted to be with someone who
Desired greatness as he did
Humph, wonder why I still remember those talks?
I hold the words close
As if I'm reciting lines from a favorite movie scene
He probably doesn't remember what he said
Or that his words would imprint on my psyche for years

My closest friends tell me I'm weird
Keeping the thoughts of these two so fresh
So alive
They say, "there are other fish in the sea"
And I say, "but none ever swim to my shore anymore"
Maybe that's why my love hasn't read the clock correctly
To my heart, today is still back then
And I'm crying
With no tears in sight
Incessantly in my mind
So much has happened between then and now
And they are still here in my mind…
He said he never made me more
Because our encounters were too
Cumbersome
I still look up that word in the dictionary
From time to time
Hoping it meant more
And that I might find my lost love in its meaning
Because that's how he summed us up
And to think
My words to sum up the other one are gone and never coming back
And to sum up me and him, the word is almost

Unconscious

When you looked at me
I had no awareness of a stare with that depth
I had no knowledge of the depth of your glare
When you asked me questions about forever
I had no awareness of the profundity of your care
Your emotional fragility struck me as bone honesty
Not vulnerability
Your attention to my life
My circumstances
But those moments I left undefined
Unweighted
When I had come to know that depth for myself
I looked back to that time
And regret filled my cavity
Oh the pain
The revelation of my unawareness
I had not known that depth for myself then

My heart aches

No one knows the pain is still here
The secret pain I hide from all, even me
My heart aches
I still believe God makes no mistakes
I reacted with anger
Frowning, taking it out on others; strangers, loved ones
It's not their fault
It's something pulling at me on the inside

Residue

I had a dream that the one I can't get over called

I was grateful, but

I balled

Cried my heart out in your ear

Even after all these years

I just couldn't let go

Just want to say thanks for thinking of me

Because my thoughts of you carried forward

Just wanted you to know how your love touched my life

I didn't choose you to be the prototype

It just happened that way

Each and every day I prayed these feelings away

And they stayed

What am I to do?

I never thought I'd see the day
When I'm in total disarray
Crying all the time
Laughing and still hurting inside
Ashamed to tell the truth
Many years later...still...
I'm not over you
What am I to do?
Try to hide and wait?
Can't throw shade to this heartache
No shelter from this pain
Gotta go through it
How long I gotta do it?
I'm embarrassed
With my own heart I was careless
I think I left it all there
Where?
Nowhere.
You never cared
I cared, so stupid
What am I to do?
I'm still hurting
Was it even worth it?
I'm still hurting
Was it worth it?

Lady sings the blues
Wish I wasn't in my shoes
What am I to do?
I never allowed myself to breakdown
Self-preservation
Tried suppressing my emotions
And they weighed me down
Slowly, each year passes

I'm not ready for you to leave

I'm not ready for you to leave
I don't know what to do
Accept it or plead?
I needed you to stay another month
Two or three
This is my problem with like or love
The bullshit sucks
You get knee-deep in
And a mofo is ready to leave
And I'm ready to coast
Enjoy you some more
And you wanna take that from me
I have some maturing and growth to do
Because I'm still not ready for you to leave

Still

I keep remembering you
Even when I'm not trying to
It's been years
I'm not still here
Romancing the idea of you and I
When we've already said goodbye
My love is so strong
Your loving is gone
And I'm still holding on
Can someone please tell me what went wrong?
Dial your number
Then hang up fast
Sick to my stomach
I have butterflies
This is crazy
I'm not yours anymore
You don't even care
Gotta get over you
Told myself this a time or two
But my love still lingers
I don't know what to do
I guess we all have unfinished business
The strongest of us all
Learn to suffocate the past
Keep it from surfacing
But me, I'm suffocating inside
I let it go and it comes back
And time and time again
I want you *still*

Abandoned

What do I say?
Not sure how I feel

I'm angry with you

But what will that do?

I needed you

You were nowhere to be found

Such a heavy load to carry on my own

You showed signs that you'd behave this way

I ignored them thinking over time we'll be okay…

But this time

Just this one time

I thought you'd come through

That hurt me deeply

I still hurt

I still cry

I still wonder why you didn't know the magnitude of your actions

What do I say?

Not sure how I feel

I'm angry with you

But what will that do?

I've tried to let it go

But it comes back, in my senses and in my being

I've tried to forget too, but that doesn't work

I think I've forgiven you

The thoughts are less

The hurt is as intense but less frequent
It's been a long time
What do I say?
Not sure how I feel
I'm angry with you
But what will that do?
I needed you
I really needed you

Funny thing is...

I wasn't ready for our love to be over
That doesn't mean it didn't need to end
But you stopped your love
While my love was still going
The unfair part is I can't just stop
I need more time
You put an end to us
A sudden disruption to my love
You're at stop and I'm still at go
What happened to meeting in the middle?
Red light, green light, no?
Let's at least get to yellow
Be fair to me
You don't want to talk anymore
Even though it hurts
My mind is still in love with you
I feel blindsided
Why didn't you keep me in the know?
I didn't have time to prepare for you to go
I don't have a problem breaking up
Just need to let love run its course
You're at one and I'm still at ten
At least give me time to get used to you not being around
We're not on bad terms
I need to let it burn
You're the cause and the cure
So I need you near

Give me another chance

Give me another chance
To put into words how I feel
When we were together
I was shocked by the truth
I fell for you after date two
I was sprung; love's hangover
I didn't know what to say
So I kept quiet
When we were over
"We" lingered for me and I couldn't deny it
But I didn't act like I cared
I didn't say what we shared,
It was special
I tried to say so
But my actions didn't confirm though
I didn't break the rules for you
Now I feel like a fool
I didn't think I'd feel so strong
So soon
Give me another chance
To show you how I feel

Invisible

I'm invisible to you
No matter how hard I try to be my best
You only appreciate my efforts
When they are possessed by someone else
And still you can't see me for seeing them
You don't appreciate me
What is wrong?
Who do I gotta be?
I take care of home
I'm domesticated, sophisticated and educated
Damn now I'm just frustrated
I'm sexy, independent
All anyone would want and more
But if you can't see me
I'm leaving
I'm in front of your face
And you can't see me
I cook, decorate and clean
I'm spiritually grounded
Stylish and astute
I'm gutter, yet strong
Ghetto in stilettos
You can't see me
I'm all that and more

Heartbreaker

You're a heartbreaker and a liar

Masterfully deceptive

Ingenious strategy

All to get to me

You used your good for evil

You see my love and the fullness thereof

And your thoughts go to taking advantage of me

But the thing is you're the one in need of love

I don't have any guards up

Because I welcome real love

But you're miserable

A closed wall

So you're looking to hurt someone

How did I get here?

How did I get here?

Oh, I remember

I was hard pressed, asunder, downtrodden

And almost succumb to the plight of hopelessness

With nowhere to turn and no one to understand

The loudness and severity of my disdain

For years the clutter in my head kept me awake at night

Secretly I'd keep it inside but the disdain manifested physically

The weight piled on pound after pound

I became more despondent

More enraged

More apathetic and ungrateful for such an arduous fate

My thoughts were ugly; the weight gain was ugly

My surroundings were ugly

My future was ugly especially if it was a reflection of my present

Ugh!

The taste of disdain is still fresh on my tongue

The anticipatory fear that it can happen again

The inaudible discomfort tinged in metallic apprehension

The taste so vivid I cringe in memoriam

But that's how I got here

I couldn't hold in my dissatisfaction with life

It bubbled into my midriff, my thighs, my buttocks, my chin, my waist, my toes

The disdain was stagnant and stale

Every day

Submerged in despair's presence like a gauze in an open wound

And yeah, I remember

When the tears fell profusely

They even stopped falling for a period of time

Then returned

Here, hurts like hell

How do I survive unrequited love?

Unrequited love will take you out

No one talks about this part

Love is as essential as water

Without it life is dry

How do you contain the thoughts of love and

Fathom its infinite expressions?

For emptiness fills empty

Loneliness feels lonely

Lovelorn strikes blow after blow

How do I survive unrequited love, the expression in the sensual?

There is a deep void in my love throne

As an unexpected yet desired kiss's imprint

Embeds its memory in my sense receptors

My love memory, the expression in the sensual is missing

I don't remember it anymore

Years have come and gone

How do I survive this loss of love expression?

I thought it'd last forever

It's been over well before the last lingering memory of it faded

How do I survive unrequited love?

I need you

That night when I called
And uttered those words
'I need you'
I meant it
You responded
"No you don't"
I thought maybe I was in my feelings
Maybe you were right...
But without you I am ruined
I now spend my days and nights
Haunted by the memory of you
Knowing that when I said
'I need you'
That was part of a premonition
An insight, a look into where I am now
It hurts
I have tried to move on
I think of you often
And I let the thought go
I let the feeling go
But the thought of you circles back
It won't go away
Because when I uttered those words
'I need you'
I meant it

I should be over you

I should be over you now
But I'm not, problem is
I don't even know how
Riddle me this
I'm strong, even keel
But this love loss I can't deal
I try mindfulness over mindless chatter
Rise above it all
In the future, you won't even matter
But what's so, is the truth
I'm falling to pieces
I was really in love with you
It's taking a while
A little longer than right now
The lingering of blue is half the battle
Losing you has my world shattered
This heartache is very clever
It has me beat, feeling depleted
Nothing left but what was…of you and me
Positive thinking
Power thoughts
So many meditation CDs I bought
Prayers and Scriptures
Front row at church
Even still, this here, hurts

Something I never want to experience again
But I'm not giving up on love
I deserve love
I want love
You can't ruin it all for me
You won't ruin it all for me
But for now
This is what's so

Idea of love

The idea of love left a long time ago
Love thoughts extinct
Just holding on to memories
Good feelings, longings and night caps
The romance left that space
And the numbness is bad
How did I get to this place?
I gotta trace my steps
Don't wanna be sad
But tears still roll down my face
How bad is bad?
When the hope for love isn't within grasp
Sad for days but numb to it all
I need love fast

Introduction

You;

You introduced this emotion to my system

Love;

Not just any love, but a love specifically of me loving you

Leave;

This love won't go

I've tried to scrub it off over and over and over

It won't go

Leave

Just because you're ready to walk away

Doesn't mean my heart stops caring and loving you that day

No, I don't want to stop

I hate you

But I love you

And I want you to stay

How selfish you didn't consult

With my heart first

My love for you lingers

Though your love for me is fleeting

My love for you remains

You let go

I'm holding on

You're over me

I'm not ready to end this love

Not yet

Where do these emotions go?

My love for you no longer has a home

I'm in shock

A state of dismay

Love reign down on my parade

You need to stay

Say the right thing

Say what I need

You cut me deep

Now help stop the bleeding

Help to stop the pain

I can't run away

It hurts on the inside

I wasn't ready to let love go

Not yet

Leftover

No one ever talks about the pain of love, not really

Well, I take that back, no one ever talks about the lovelornness that doesn't leave

Just because everyone says, "get over it"

Doesn't mean I'm over it

I'm pissed

I'm lost

Road less traveled

I'm a failure at love

The pain is still fresh

Like a knife pierced into my flesh

There's an immovable scar

Are there any books for me?

Are there any quotes for me?

Can anyone hear me?

I can't talk to anyone about this anyway

They'll never understand

Mind over matter, right?

This will never end

Other love has come since

None has lasted

I'm ruined

Why did I ever open my heart?

I'm still grieving your absence

I'm ashamed to mention how long it's been

I see you in my dreams even

I still see things that remind me of you

I still remember your phone number

This is denial

The connection we once had has to mean something

You already told me

"No it doesn't"

But my heart still hopes

It's as if I don't think you really knew

So I hope for you and me too

It is over

Those three words are hard to bear

If only I had known that letting you in

Was forever for me

But for never for you

A

It's a year later

I'm still here

Thought I'd crossed this bridge

But unh uh, love doesn't play fair

This love affair was

A contradiction

A misadventure

A joy ride

A sweet addiction

A pleasure thrill

A kinky high

How can I love someone I don't really like?

I don't know

But I enjoyed the moments

And the things we did

Stay

I don't know the words to say to make it right
You and I are behind
I don't know what to do to get you off my mind
Sometimes I cry because when I close my eyes
All I see is you and me
This can't be happening
I want to be free
My mind says hell no
You ain't worth another thought
But my heart says yes
And I pick up the phone to call
What is the balance?
Cause I can't have this back and forth
Remembering all the pain that you left me
I feel so empty
You're not present
But your love taunts me
And I stay for another go round

It_hurts@forward

You were my ideal

The prototype

I knew deep down inside this rejection would be different

Because your rejection

Rejected the notion of who I saw as a mate for me

I gave you my highest stamp of approval

I thought you were my reflection

I spend the years learning to be open to love again

I know this was me falling in love alone

Loving someone who didn't love me back

I love hard, and like Siddhartha

When I see something I want I go after it

The same way a pebble rushes to the bottom of the ocean floor

I'm finding my way back

Marred by the pain

Had I known then what I know now

I would've never let our incipient affair flourish into more in my mind

If you didn't love me

Why did our lovemaking reach uninhabited spaces?

Why didn't another have the same power?

What was so significant about you?

Did I let you become something that neither of us wanted?

I'm not

I'm not a keeper huh?
Well you lied to me
Did you tell your secret?
You said you're a divorcée
Who knew you were playing games
You made me sin and disrespect your family
I would hurt you but I don't want a felony offense
You never said you were married
See, I care about being faithful
I want your family to last
Clearly more than you do
I'm not a homewrecker
I'm not
You lied

No commitment

I can't say those 3 words
Falling for you is unheard of
When I'm alone
I'm owning my own
But with you in the picture
Things are wrong
Is it you or me?
I usually know what makes me happy
At least I think
I won't let go
The words won't come out
Maybe I have too much pride
I don't know if I need you in my life
Don't wait for me to say I love you first
Don't expect me to pressure you about marriage
I don't know which would be worse
I don't want either and there is nothing wrong with me needing my independence
I'm not going to say I love you and resent it
I love you
Nah, I'm not saying it
I'm scorn
My love is in a vault
Torn between was it yours, or my fault
You should keep moving

I...love...I love you
Nah, I can't do it
I ain't in no spouse mood
I'm chillin'
Everybody not trying to be settled
I'm doing my own thing
Maybe in the future
Serious relationships can be a heavy load
Those three words won't come out
I'll feel like I've lost control
Not sure the cause of it
But I don't want no commitment

Train wreck

My love has to go
It's getting on the train at high noon
And soon the door is gonna close
So you better get here
Or you better get there
Real fast
Super fast
Leave time to pay fare
Because my love is leaving soon
I've waited and wondered
So confused
I gave myself the blues
Thinking…
Was it me?
Was it you?
Or was I the one who played the fool?
Now it's all good
My composure's cool
Packing my bags
Because my love is leaving soon
Oh, how I loved you
But the door is closing
You, me, we won't be the focus
Hurry the door is closing
Time is running out

All fears and doubts
All leaving rapidly
Gotta get there fast
Don't believe me?
The door is closing
Time is up
My love is leaving
By the way
I took the bus!

Flower brigade

I'm not letting you in
I'll love you from afar instead
So your words don't hurt
I have to block it all
Even your love
Because your faults are unpredictable
I don't want to hurt anymore
I'm not letting you in
I'll love you from afar instead
What a dead end and a newly paved road
If I have faith I'll learn to forgive those before you
But then the pain flashes and I'm cold again
Where do I begin?
Again.
I'm not letting you in
I'll love you from afar instead

Traffic light

How am I to face tomorrow?
No longer yours
How do I remake me over in an hour?
This is messed up
You give me no choice
I wish you'd allow me to get to yellow
Before you let go
This is messed up
You give me no choice
Green light
Yellow light
Red.

Let me go!

Let me go

You've tortured me long enough

You've depressed my senses

Lured me into a state of dismay

Became a nuisance

Your loveless-ness is past tense

Stop trying to hurt me now

You didn't want me

We're not meant to be

You won't want me in the future either

There are no more possibly-s

I've held captive that idea so long

My heart doesn't know happiness

My heart is comfortable with sadness

Was that your goal?

To destroy my love cells?

Well you won

Because I surrender to all love lost

Double jeopardy

My heart can't break twice for the same heartache

Let me go

You can't hold me to a past that has passed

I want to love

I have courage to love again

Part III: MEDIUM GRIT

Sandpaper with Medium Grit removes small imperfections and marks.

Henceforth

At the breaking point of despair and giving up

Plump opaque tears on my eyelashes

Distorting my view

Beading from my lower eyelids...

Tears rush down my cheeks

And in exasperation, that frightful thin line

You *know* that thin line

A glimmer of hope springs forth

And for the first time in months

In weeks, in days

I remember me before the breakup

Before I was overwhelmed and lost in my thirst for love

I remembered me and all that I was before, during and henceforth

In due time

As I stood on the veranda I could see the sunrise

I could see the wilderness burgeoning in the distance

As I began my journey, I packed light, carrying very little

I needed to be near the river by dusk

As I made my way, fear set in and I was unsettled

I panicked midway and frantically started running back to the veranda

Because from there, I could see my destination

I could smell the scent of accomplishment

I could taste the fresh river water

I could feel the coolness of the flow

See my reflection in the fresh river water

Because from the veranda, I had hope, I could see my destination

It wasn't until I started to trek the terrain

When I couldn't see a destination from endless wilderness

Trees, spiders, moss, snakes;

All my fears rushed in like an unexpected wind

I fell to my knees

Clasped my face in my hands and I sobbed

Torn from the desire to reach the river and from fear, both paralyzed my movement

I lay there until nightfall

Trembling, afraid, anxious, ashamed, sad and feeling alone

I sat holding my knees in my arms for hours in pure agony;

Feeling rodents and insects tickle my flesh until goose bumps sprang up like a heaving rash

And acceptance thrust my body into shock, numbness

I had no choice but to wait for the stars to fade as the color of night turned light blue

Then when sunrise came, I was exhausted from night

All I could hope was that someone would see me

Someone on their way to the river would find me

Help me get to the river, too

I begged and pleaded with God

Send someone to come get me

I can't go at it alone

As I mustered enough strength to get back on the path

I crawled

Then walked for hours

Still afraid

Startled by the slightest sound of twig or leaf rustling

As I made one last attempt to go forward

My knees buckled below me

I saw a silhouette at the end of my eyesight

His flesh looked just as worn

I sat for a while

Keeping my eyes perched on him as much as possible

My visibility waned from time to time

Then I started walking in his direction

Once we came upon one another there was a sigh of relief

We embraced each other

Then standing side by side

Our arms interlocked

We took our gaze off each other

We looked out and just ahead we could see the river

We helped pull each other over a log

We had made it to the river, together

Inward

Looking into your eyes
Reminds me of what I dream for
Looking into your eyes
Let's me know I deserve love
Looking into your eyes
Makes me forget about the bad times
Looking into your eyes
Gives me happiness that can't be paid for
Looking into your eyes
Was more intense than any touch
Looking into your eyes
Stabilized me to my core
Looking into your eyes
I knew the meaning of true love
Even though the sun sets on our love
You're irreplaceable
Even though we're no more
At one moment I shared a love space with you
Even though you're another's now
What we had means even more
In my heart is where our love lived
That's where our capacity to love one another was built
Sincere adornment
You kept my love tank on full
It was true love

Love again

They were just words you said
But they shredded my heart like fray
It was just another decision for you
But it left me broken and unsure
By now you've moved on
But what was between us it continues on
Keeping me from taking another chance at love
To you it wasn't a good look
As if I fell in love with you on my own
It takes two
I wonder if you led me on
I take credit for my part
You don't care at all
Told me to be responsible for my own heart
With that how do I keep from falling apart?
I can't let this go on any longer
I gotta dial in and remember me before you
Getting over you is my new hunger
I must be free to love again
I'm going to love again
And forget about you

I thought it was me

You looked into my eyes
I pictured the rest of our lives
You complimented my beauty
Even said I had nice thighs
You touched my legs once or twice
Discussed thoughts of loving me
What a surprise, what a surprise
You talked about what if
What if it was you and I?
And you thought I wouldn't know
You were feeding me some mess
You only planned to be my friend
You've got someone else
Why is it this way?
The one of my dreams
Already gave someone else my ring
Well, what, why and
How did we get to this?
You brought the pain again
You asked someone else for their hand in marriage

Not #1

There is something eerily soothing in knowing
You're not the first to break my heart
If you'd been the blueprint it would have hurt much worse
You are still the formidable challenge later in life
To remind me
Just how much I've overcome lost love
Before you

Expectations

After years of independence, Marly succumbed to love's dictatorship. And not just any old dictatorship but the need for love. Marly realized her need for love; for companionship, even if incomplete, uncertain and painful, because not having love felt worse.

Therefore, her relationship with Ali was satisfactory at best. With all its' loose ends and idiosyncrasies - once she settled in her heart what she really needed, she decided she wouldn't think of it as settling. Settling to her, was not allowing the heart what it wanted and desired for so long.

Instead, Marly let it be. She let the relationship define itself and she decided to be open to its offerings and adjusted her expectations so she was no longer disappointed. At the baseline, Marly just needed company, someone to ask, it didn't matter at this point how much they cared, "How are you?" If not every day, at least ask any day.

Now, from here Marly could build by using this relationship to fill the gap; the lowly pit of lovelessness. This relationship would catapult Marly out of the lowly pit to the surface where she could search for love without being on empty at the start.

Unfaithful

I'm a good person
I don't cause no drama
I don't break up happy homes
Learned that from my mama
If they knew about you
How it's not my fault
I'm falling in love that is true
But you're a liar too
Now I've got to shake you off
And find my way through
I'm so angry
You leave my house
Go home to another
How could you let this be?
Cheating is exponentially hurtful *after* sex
Thankfully I *didn't* give you the goods
I'm pissed with you
I was intrigued by you
But I never gave too much because I observed you
Why would you tease me?
I was daydreaming about the future us
Thank God I didn't give it up
I'd be tripping
Flipping out on you
I feel hateful
I can't believe you're unfaithful

When you gone

When you gone
The fireworks show is ending, the grand finale
When you gone
All that's right is wrong
When you gone
The lyre plays the music to my song
When you gone
I ain't even gotta hold my tongue
When you gone
I can finally move on

What do you want from me?

What do you want from me?
If you don't want nothing you'll regret it
If you want something you won't regret it
Feeling as low as low can be
I have all to give and none to give, you see
Oxymoronic
Slow speed
High valley
The depth and height reminds me to ask
What do you want from me?
If you don't want nothing you'll regret it
If you want something you won't regret it
Seize my highs and my lows
Unequivocally this is all of me
A drought and wellspring
So, what do you want from me?
If you don't want nothing you'll regret it
If you want something you won't regret it

Analogy

Tree leaves
Breeze, breeze
Rainstorm, brainstorm
Commonly
Watering tree leaves
Watering me think
Lightning strikes, life strikes
Broken leaves, broken me
Tornado, breakdown
Trees upside down, me upside down
Silent trees
Me, I scream

Love you in wonderment

Not choosing you
When you asked me
Is my biggest regret to date
I was afraid
I thought I had more time to decide
Back then I was running from love
All the time
I knew I wanted you deep down
But I let you go
I can't ever tell you though
It would destroy so much
Maybe even keep you away, forever.
She deserves you more, anyways
Because when you chose her she chose you too
I rest in the fact that fate might've determined that life for you
I wonder, not too often, but every blue moon
What life would be like
If I had the courage and the hindsight to let you love me
And I reciprocate
Just maybe…
No, I won't go there because I'm not waiting, just wondering
Sometimes I smile because I know that someone as special as you
Wanted me

And that's enough for me to keep going but
I wonder, not too often, but every blue moon
What would be different if I chose you too
And I close this thought
Because I can't change what's so
Instead I'll love you in wonderment
That nonexistent place

55 days in

Here we go again
Thought it all be ended by now
I'm a little frustrated
Not one date in
Solely communication
Not really empty promises
Just not sure how much to invest
Hopes for future happenings
Reminisces of past hurts recycling
Kinda want you to be leavin'
But that's not quite the reason
Just not wanting you here like this
Too much uncertainty
And I'm anxious again
Trying to be a 'let it flow' kinda person
Why can't I let this be?
Because of the vulnerabilities
I want to let my feelings free
Latch on to you while you're in my space
But I'm back on the fence again
Wondering will you disappear
Not your fault my mind goes here again
And end this romancipation
And out of fear I want you to go
While I'm anticipating it

Not sure why you're still here
I'm puzzled but it's too soon to be
Asking all these questions
I'll give you more time
Just a little though
And I'll keep questioning should I stay or let it go
Maybe it'll go past summer
Maybe we'll begin something new
What the hell
Every text I grin and grin and grin
And we're only 55 days in

Dreams birthed

For years the tears fell not
For years my heart felt not
Worried
Suppressing reality is harmful to my existence
In my resistance
I listened
The vision tarried
Faint not
Is the talent alive?
Is the gift viable?
Do I even believe? In me? In God? In my gift?
The sound of birthing is the sound of crying
And I weep

Don't forget love

I was numb for longer than I realized

My heart was broken in more places than I could mend on my own

Without my own admonition I surrendered the possibility of love again

I couldn't find the courage to love again that Dr. Angelou speaks of

I had forgotten where love resonates in my body

Without knowing, the idea of love visited recently

And like an intruder or foreign cell

My love antibodies attacked and I've been angry

Emotionally unstable, rebellious and disappointed in myself for letting the idea of love resuscitate itself in my being

The feelings were so unfamiliar I couldn't sleep

I felt warmth and angst in my stomach

My thoughts raced

Bracing myself for the worst

Heartbreak, *again*?

Desiring the incorrigible fate of numbness which was more normal and welcomed in my system, then

One random morning the idea of love paraded in my cells and danced in my body

As usual I was ready to be uneasy and on the defensive

But as I exhaled in the moment

I realized the idea of love was home, resettled

Welcomed in my soul not as an intruder or foreign cell

But as an old companion

And we picked up where we left off like no time had lapsed

Part IV: FINE GRIT

Sandpaper with Fine Grit is the final sanding before finishing.

Sit-in

Oh, I've tried to cover up, hush up all of life's pain and disappointment

Every heartache I've tried to heal with life's ointment

I ate and I spent and I ate and I spent

And I isolated and vented

But it never went away

For I have tried to run from it all

Silently overeating but starving

Trying to kill it but I was the only one dying inside

Then I started to protest myself

The ways I had avoided life's feelings and emotions

I called on all emotions from here and there

I called internal judges and lawyers to plead my case

Because I was turning myself in

For I needed justice

I needed to stop being on the run

To stop eating and spending whenever I became undone

It was time to mend

So I decided to protest with a sit-in

I will sit through

Every uncomfortable moment

Every painful circumstance

Every sorrowful situation

Even the unhappy occasions

The protest has begun with a sit-in

Onward

I stand at the precipice of knowledge, historical perspective and classics

Onward as each quote strewn all over the sky, like contrails, that lead to the hill I see in the distance

Onward as each poem fills in the designs of my architectural blueprint

Onward as each short story relishes the ease with which others write

The lucid freedom in a box that is no longer a box but a beat up wall

Individuality misconfigured that box

Onward as each novel illuminates the path toward inward chambers held hostage with lock and key

Onward the words act as a zoom in, zoom out function where I can see the hilltop and below are all the writers, without genre, without a box

Clutter

Attic
Attic
That's where my thoughts have been
That *is* where my thoughts have been
Matter
Matter
That's where my heart has been
That *is* where my heart has been
Clutter
Clutter
That's where my silence has been
That *is* where my voice has been

Grandeur

Grandeur moments
That's what I'm living for
Grandeur stages
That's what I'm striving for
Grandeur joy
That's what I'm praying for
Grandeur love
That's what I'm breathing for
Grandeur passion
That's what I'm giving for
Grandeur sights
That's what I'm working for
Grandeur tastes
That's what I'm lusting for
Grandeur me
That's what I'm waiting for

Giving

I am a writer

Didn't always believe so

It took many goads from God

I am a poet

I am a thinker

I second guess a lot

I am learning to love

I am learning to forgive

Every day

I am an emotional mess

I am scar tissue

Healing

I am a legacy of humility

And love

I am gospel music to the core

Praise is what I do and prayer too

I am hip hop beats

Sometimes secretly depending on the crowd

I stopped that shit though

Now I just be me

Because I don't like all music neither

So no need to be pretending

I don't have to hide my preferences no more

I am keen to stop cursing

"Don't let your affliction reflect in your diction," says Coach

I am spontaneity

I don't like suspense

I am a dreamer

God please don't take away unused talents

I pray

Often, a lot

Fearful, hopeful, believe so

I am imagination

Exaggerated versions of everything

I am my parents' daughter

Authentic, painful addictions

Loving; good people, givers

I am at the ocean now

Actually, always there somehow

I am inspired

My soul jumps

Wisdom cries out

God breathed inspiration

Can't understand it

Pray. No answer. Psalm 31:7

I am not fond of multitasking

One big task, two maybe, more if smaller okay

I am an in-the-car-by-myself-concert singer

Practicing hard, every day

I am alive

Aware, hypersensitive, vulnerable, reinventing, wondering...

I am underdeveloped strength
It peaks, peers when needed most
I am here
1980. Detroit. Motown. Seven Mile Road
Oh, most importantly
I am a very grateful person; very grateful
I'm learning to give more
You're welcome!
I am passive
Avoiding stereotypical anger
Usually I go 0 to 100
I am learning assertive, finding my 50
I am resisting;
Violent TV, negative messages, technology
I don't always know where my phone is
Addictive, overconsuming
I am not trusting. I don't trust them
The uneducated mostly
Those in 1800s, them in 1968
Unless I see God in them
Almost fearful
It's hatred, different evil-spirit type
I pray hard. Hard
I cry, remembering Jesus wept
I am learning to forgive
I am still learning to love
Every day

I am learning that I can love or fear, but choose only one
I am angry, sometimes
I hold too much in
I judged the protector within
That hurt
Now I'm fair to myself
I must say so when words hurt
Acknowledging at least therein lies freedom
Now working on the middle
I am free

Significance

I now realize I don't want to let go

That space was one of the most imperfectly complete times of my life

I surrendered to love on my terms

I don't want to forget it all

I gave all I had

I did

No regrets

So I'll tuck away the memories without regret and pain

The world isn't the same without you

But nothing is the same anyways

Instead of what I've lost

You allowed me to tap into emotions I never knew before you were here

And that is the beauty of it all

Your significance is obtrusive

Moving on

Even though you're walking down that aisle
Nothing can erase the times you made me smile
I don't regret it
I'm not even upset
I'm just happy that we shared love
That we knew each other this lifetime
That is something no one or nothing can take away
Not even your wedding day
Good life, love
Know that I'm not sad
You gave me closure
At the ordained time it was over
This ain't no sad song
It's a love song
The now for us is a now for you two
And I'm moving on
I'm standing tall
Knowing I loved you, I can love another
Knowing you loved me, means I can be loved
Thank you for the time we had together
It ain't over for me
Love lives on
Love goes on
Love survives

Believe in me

I'm not giving up believing in me
I have a dream
A desire on the inside of me to do great things
So what's at the heart of it all?
Believing in me
I can achieve
No negative thinking
Just believe

I am single

Calling me every day, "What you doing?"
I don't want that
Fussing because someone called me cutie
I don't want that
Holding me and cuddling
I don't want that
Buying my food taking me out feeling macho
I don't want that
In my face while tennis is on
I don't want that
Asking when the food'll be done
I don't want that
Having a relationship is not my only dream you know
Getting a diamond ring
I can buy my own things
The pressure and questions about being single
Being single is an enjoyable season
Ain't no need to rush
This is my life
I don't want to spend the most of my years
Being a spouse
What about my destiny and what I need to do
I got better things to do like write a book, travel the world, be a better friend
What about you?

Chill

"Can we be friends?"
Yes that's cool with me
Just need to know
That's all it is
And I'll put you in the friend box quick
And go on about my business
But how do I find this out?
I don't like suspense
And most people can chill until further notice
But I'm an anxious person
Longer story...
I need the suspense to be over in a hurry
Just let me know the deal
Then I can chill

Conscious

I had not known the depth for myself then

I felt fraught with despair

I realized timing was more the matter

For my unawareness then

Created my awareness now

Impeccable timing

At this juncture

The perfect one, not then or before

But now

When you look at me

I am aware of your stare

Such depth in your glare

When you ask me questions about forever

I feel the care

Your emotional fragility is love

Sincere and honest

Your attention to my life, my circumstances

Like a mirror

We share in the depth

Like déjà vu

You're here now and I'm aware

You get to there

You get to there
You really do
But how is the matter of the fact
Some nights and days and even more nights
I cried
Sometimes the tears wouldn't flow
They were nowhere to be found
So I had to sit and endure and agonize
And use vices and become angered
Unsettled, broken
Heart ached; stress riveted my body and took on so many forms
I didn't recognize myself and I wasn't always fun to be around
I was snappy and I was mean
I let others walk all over me
There was no justice
The world and its people were unkind and unfair
Pause
Now that my nights and days are no longer that way
I have perspective
I've learned just how low I'm willing to go
I learned my bottom, my baseline
And now I know that even at my bottom
I have to be fair to me
What's even more beautiful is I now know

That my expectations...

Well I no longer attach expectations on anything outside of my baseline

And that perspective is how I let people be

See I must expect at all times to be fair to myself, now, at least

But at the bottom, at the baseline, at the low place

My inner protector will be there, always

That's the expectation!

Not that no one will ever be unkind and unfair

But that even in the nights and days that are too long to bear

I expect me to be kind and fair and protective of me

And even though the night was tough

My new perspective was worth every second

Every minute of my agony and my despair

You get to there

You really do

Figure it out

Trying to figure it all out
Fit into the box designed by everyone else
Fighting through the maze of doubt
I have dreams and goals
But where do they fit?
I can't easily say I'm a doctor or a lawyer
Or a hippy or a sommelier
Why can't my answer be easier?
Or circular or even triangular
After all, why are you asking if you really don't care?
I'm passionate about my thoughts
And emotional healing
Traveling the world
Meeting many people at my leisure
Working to end homelessness
And writing a novel
Statistical analysis and research
Cooking veggies and eating fruit
Living and playing in water
And dancing until my feet hurt
These are my passions
All that's on my to-do list
And no it's not one word or a one liner
But frankly dear, I don't give a shit
It's my life and what I want to do!
And no longer will I shrink when I tell you

Love circle

As Korin stood in front of Jake in the kitchen, the tears rolled down her cheeks. She was so frustrated and angered. Korin had been holding in her emotions for years now and while she had no idea how this was going to come out, she still wanted it to come across with love, direct but with finesse, because at the root of it all, was love. Both Jake and Korin loved each other in ways that only they knew. Jake contended that he'd been unhappy. Korin seemed so distant at times. Something wasn't right and so maybe they should take a break. Korin's heart shattered at such talk, and she couldn't hold it in any longer.

"Jake, I mean well when I say this, but I fight so hard every day not to run. I'm good at running from love. Actually I'm better at running from love than I am at staying in love. I am fighting to stay here right now because running is easier." She continued, "running is my norm; this makes me so uncomfortable. I am so afraid of how much I love you more and more each day. That fear is paralyzing and it renders me powerless.

I am most vulnerable to you in a way that I have never been. And the sheer thought that at any moment you could walk out that door and take away this love that I fight for, that I nurture, that I pray for, that I am scared shitless of, but I put myself in the ring every night and I fight not to run. I fight to stay here and love you. So to hear those words that I'm distant, that you need a break. That my dear is music to my ears because that is the easy way out for me. But what we have, what we've created, what is even stronger than my fear of loving you to the point of no return, is that our love is good.

Our love is real. Love lives in us. I love you, Jake. See that's the problem. I love you and I don't know how to love you without the fear of loving you. The fear of loving you so much that if you leave, you will take a part of me that I can't get back. I'm not distant Jake – I know it may come across that way, but I'm closer to you than you'll ever know. Because when I say I love you, I mean it in a way that is so strong, so endearing, and so authentic; I love you wholly."

Jake looked at Korin, who had turned toward the sink, leaning over it, sobbing. With every fiber of emotion in his body he rushed to Korin and held her and kissed her and apologized. "I had no idea you were so afraid. I guess, I'm afraid too. And that makes two of us too afraid to lose each other and the love we have," he said. Jake looked into her eyes and talked to her heart. "I'm in this too. Korin I'm not running unless you run, and even then we'll run from whatever this is and simply call it something else, together."

Peace

I want a *peace* of my own
Standing in muddy waters
Or up ole shits creek
I want *peace*
I want a *peace* of my own

Part V: EXTRA FINE GRIT

Sandpaper with Extra Fine Grit polishes surfaces.

New

As exotic as a thunderstorm during a white winter
As unfamiliar as an untried spice on the palate

What is this love?

What is this love?

That churns the spirit

Ringing out the grittiness of life

What is this love?

When the spirit is in agony

A silent pain so loud

And also untouchable

When the pain subsides

The release of the pressure presents a beauty

An indescribable empathy

Experienced by each in its own way

What is this love?

That creates a longing of forever, safety and happiness

The desire for another to live a better life

The best life

What is this love?

That brings the dead back to life, Lazarus

Or snaps someone from the past and future

To feel so intently present

What is this love?

Even in the moment of overexertion

Passion, anger or danger

Reminds you that your own humanity matters

Everybody's humanity matters

What is this love?

That will enable your breath to coexist
With that of a bad person
That allows breath to fill the lungs and life
Of your cavity and theirs
Maybe this love suggests a continuity of love that is nonjudgmental or practical
What is this love?
That connects us on a visceral level
The leaping when we sense a kindred spirit
A wisdom that cries out
Hinting to the beauty and talent within
What is this love?

Scars

As I look through the bars of a jail cell

My imagination tunes out the rustic cement and angry mirror of stares

Instead I look into a field of flowers, lowly

So I can see a pretty girl dancing in the distance

I move from bar to bar in my cell as if to get a better look

The girl is mesmerizing; all the passersby are looking curiously with amazement

The girl's smile is so bright it's unearthing

Her skin looks so smooth and radiant

Her natural coif and black eyebrows are as shiny as a raven's feather

She dances and her movements so refined and quick, I look for a drummer

Her skin looks beautiful like it has been dipped in bronze

When she lifts her arms, her shirt rises exposing a scar

It was sizable but it doesn't take away from her beauty

It makes her more beautiful because the scar exposes her mortality

At first she skipped a movement when she noticed her scar was exposed

But with her left hand she touched the scar with a few finger tips

In a manner as if there was blood present or a deep gash

Then with slight dismissal

She dropped her left hand from her belly

Wrapped her right hand around the scar and kept dancing

She kept dancing

Freestyle

Wind blows
Calming breeze
Tides turn
Washed ashore
Rescued at last
Familiarity?
It's different this time

Reach!

Reach for more
Reach and soar
Reach beyond the moment
Reach within so you can own it
Reach!
Reach into your soul
Reach and find love
Reach beyond the second guessing
Reach inside and there's your blessing
Reach into your heart
Reach!
Reach and find the meaning
Reach until you get what you want
Reach and learn the lesson
Reach so you don't run
Reach so you see what's waiting
When you make it over the doubt
That's kept you from reaching
Reach!
Reach above defeat
Reach to the clouds
Reach over every mountain
Reach through to who you really are
Reach!
Reach you can do it
Reach you're almost to it
Reach your way through it
Reach and endure it
Reach and find yourself
Reach!

At the heart of it

Freedom is waiting for me to crack the code

Liberty is waiting for me to live life and soar

Joy is waiting for me to embrace the journey

And God is waiting for me to live life now so I'll experience eternity

So what's at the heart of it all?

My purpose

I depend upon *knowing it* to move forward

Only now matters

This very moment is all I have

And now is at the heart of it all

Dream cloud

My dream cloud
Is far in the sky
No one understands
The goals I have inside
Some laugh and make fun
Just wait 'til I overcome
I want the world to see
That I can achieve
Hard work and persistence
Perseverance and resilience
Success is at my reach
Some days are a struggle
I just want to give up
But deep inside I hear a voice
'You can make it, fight temptation'
Then courage resumes
The power exudes and now I'm on my way
Trials and tribulations
Don't determine my situation
Wait for my outcome
I will hear, "Well done!"

Fellowship

I look up at the sunshine
I look up at the stars in the sky
I look at the glass half full
I even look up at the moon
I hold my head up high
I want to think of good times, good days
Because trouble is gonna come
And we're not promised an easy road
I look up
I hold my head up
To lighten every load
I need a brighter day
I need my joy sustained
I need to feel free
I need my soul to leap
I need my mind clear so God's voice I hear
I need the clutter gone
I need to sing my song
My God speak to me
I need to hear what You say
I need to fold my hands and bend my knees
I need to pray

Saturday

Hummingbirds and blue birds

The sound of music chirps

Gallivanting in the sunlight

Taking walks

Enjoying hikes

Driving down the highway

Miles and miles nothing in our way

Mountain views

AM/FM tunes

Hair blowing in the wind

Skin browning from the sun

What an afternoon to have some fun

I've got to get to You, God

I've got to get to You, God

I'm not even sure how

Hallelujah, bless Your name Lord

It's been a while

But I remember the last time I worshiped with You

The moment was real, pure and true

And I was caught up in You, Lord

And I haven't been the same since

I'm not sure if the way I got to You last time will work this time

But I'll lift up my hands for I know You're still mine

Hallelujah, bless Your name Lord

I've got to get to You, God

I need to hear Your Word

There is healing in Your Presence

There is a blessing in every lesson

The real me, I'll find in You

I've got to get to You, God

I'm not even sure how

Hallelujah, bless Your name Lord

They say praise will illuminate the route

It's been a while but I remember the last time I worshiped You

I was caught up in You, Lord, and I haven't been the same since

I've got to get to You, God

Growth

I'm older, wiser and emotionally secure now

So I'm not giving away my love to anyone irresponsible

Only to the mature, experienced in love who know what they are getting into

No more crushing

No more rushing

No more mistaking attraction for interest

No more mistaking lust for love

Wonder

My heart beats with reverberations of you
Your call to love requires us all to reach from the depths
From which only God beholds
A life full of love
Cancels all wrongs
Heals all hearts from the hurts
That'll go far beyond you and me
I love you,
You and you
We can love our way through
Every season
Every believer
Every reason given is why I love you,
You and you
I aspire to inspire and uplift truth
If we hold love to be God's desire for our lives
Let's let love be
Reach beyond your sight
Fight off hate with all your might
Release love
Cry for all mankind
Within your embrace
You can eradicate tyranny and fear
If love is what you give
Love is what you get
So I love you,
You and you

The words

It's our words
Really
That matter
We talk all the time
It's what we write that reminds us of
The words;
With words God spoke life
It's the words that matter
The words I tell, I write

I look for You

Sometimes I look for You to step from behind the mountains

Sometimes I look at the sky waiting for You to make Your face appear and Your hands play with the clouds making figurines to capture my amazement

Sometimes I look at the ocean and think at any moment I'll see You in the distance walking toward me from the horizon

Sometimes I look at the rain and wonder if I'd see Your big feet splashing the puddles as You walk around

At night, I even look up in the sky at the stars and moon wondering if You'd make a funny face at me then too

Sometimes I look at the sun and as my eyes burn and my vision wanes I wonder if that's Your hiding place

Sometimes I stare at lightning and I wonder if the light is just bright enough to reveal exactly where You are and end our game of hide-and-seek

EPILOGUE

May

After a while; plea after plea and mellifluous tear after tear, I felt lighter, and better able to *do*. After each prayer and conversation with God, I would notice a growing pile of ash-like material. It was tan in color, like sawdust or sand, less like burned wood. Finally, when the pile got too large to ignore, I asked God what the pile was for?

In effect, God said, "Every time you prayed, I heard your plea and I saw your tears and because you called on Me for help, once you tarried for a little while and you learned to feel your emotions and be present, I started to smooth out your rough edges. I gave you beauty for your ashes." And I smiled because I knew in my spirit that I was transformed.

And I said, "God the beauty must be my perspective, my understanding because I can reflect and marvel at the courage it took to get me here." Now I can sift through the ashes, look at the pain directly and feel the emotions.

So, this time when I experience the emotions, as I hope you will too, I won't be stuck or in pain. Feeling is how we share in humanity – love, fear, hope, joy, and sorrow, are all part of the human experience.

Inspiration for book title

"The Spirit of the Sovereign Lord is on me...
He has sent me to bind up the brokenhearted...
to comfort all who mourn and provide for those
who grieve in Zion – to bestow on them a crown of beauty
instead of ashes, the oil of joy instead of mourning and a
garment of praise instead of a spirit of despair..."

(Isaiah 61:1-3)

I must be what I want you to become…
And so, I strive to be my best for you:

Christopher, David, Kayla, Xavier, Milani, Nora, Breeya, Alyssa, Brooklyn, Brooke, Madison, Jacob, Dwayne, Aidan and AnnaLynn

For the late Mar'Kesha Harrison. We miss you.

About the author

Growing up in a vibrant, protective and nurturing neighborhood on the west side of Detroit in the 80s sets the landscape for Ravenn Moore's strong connection to ethos in her debut book, *Sandpaper*. A vivid dreamer, and out-the-box thinker, Ravenn began writing at a very early age, even selling such 3 or 4 sentence works to neighbors who willingly, and lovingly bought multiple pages for at least a quarter every time she knocked on their doors.

It was there, on the west side of Detroit, where Ravenn developed an eclectic mix of grit, emotional intelligence, a sense of community; love of self and community, and a relentless grind, all eloquently conveyed between the lines of every poem in *Sandpaper*.

Ravenn received her bachelor's degree in Journalism from The Ohio State University, and a master's degree in Public Policy from the University of Chicago. Ravenn is a published journalist, copy editor and proofreader, grant writer, creative writer and financial budgeting consultant. She has worked for multiple companies and organizations in the United States and in Japan. She started Paperthick Publishing to publish her multiple collections of poetry, short stories, and novels. Ravenn also plans to publish the works of other writers as well. Ravenn resides in Detroit.

Acknowledgments

To everyone who bought this book, I am humbled. Thank you from the bottom of my heart. It is an honor to share this work with you.

Asha, I would not have written this book without you. Your interest in my work, your belief in my talent and your encouragement is truly what got me to write *Sandpaper*. I didn't know where to start then God let us cross paths. So, words will never convey my deepest gratitude for you and your role in this work. Thanks for leading the way and being an example to follow! Thank you so much, Asha Veal Brisebois! Muah!

Valerie A. Congdon, your love and support is invaluable. You are an amazing and intelligent woman and EDITOR!! You're my friend, mentor, inspiration, family – all that and more. Thank you for believing in me and helping make *Sandpaper* the best it could be. I love you!! Thanks, Val!

Tanya Garrett, you believed in me from day one. Your friendship, encouragement and insights brightened the path to me publishing *Sandpaper*. Thank you!

To my family: Aunty Karen, Aunty Betty, Aunty Pam, Uncle Champ, Uncle Gary, Uncle Jeffrey, James (Bim) and all my cousins. Thank you to my siblings: Kjea, Danielle, LaCharie, Raymon, Ashley (SJP), LaKeia, Chara and Muni.

To my bonus parents: Clyde (Coach) and Diane James, Sandra and Greg Union, Carol Haggard, Cassandra and Gilbert Thrasher, and the late L.C. Bowman (God-daddy) – I cannot imagine life without your love and support.

To my entire Faust Avenue family: The Hayes, The Turners, The Gayes, The Byrds, The Loves, The Wallaces, The Taylors, The Johnsons, The Thomas's, The Fitzgeralds,

The Barrs, The Hankins, and The Howards – your love and affections will carry me my lifetime. A child could not have dreamed for a better village. I love y'all!!

To my extended village: Darthula (Aunt Dot) Young, Kelly and Craig Myree, Aunty Vonyia and family, Linda Garrett, Karen J. Clark, Sheila McCall, Valerie and Marc Congdon, Future Mae Craig Bacon, Janice and Berry Samuel, Juanita and Deon Simmons, Jig, Tim and Wendy Rickett, Aunty Louzine and family, Tootsie and family, Aunty Niecey and Uncle Jerry, and Rev. Lawrence J. London – thanks for your love and support over the years!

Extra special thank you to Kimberly, Heidi L., Nicole (Nicks), Jenn Mikes, Shelly, Brad, Enixa, Nnamdi, Sakara, Shawvon, Suzanne, Willie, Eboni, Alana, Viana (Nan), Lisa Shumaker, Dennis (John), James, Larissa (Reese), Keyen, Shantelle, John (Man), Cemeré, Chauncey, Diondra (Dee Dee), Cubaes, Japan Crew, Ken F., Jacqueline L-E., and Jacqueline M. Thank you to my extended family, friends and educators.

Again, to my editor Valerie A. Congdon your input and support made this book possible, thank you! To Kimberly N. Simmons, thank you! To my volunteer readers, thank you! To the most talented Rose Lowry, thanks for turning my vision into art!

www.ingramcontent.com/pod-product-compliance
Lightning Source LLC
Chambersburg PA
CBHW020615300426
44113CB00007B/657